The Fifteen Mysteries
In Image and Word

M. Basil Pennington, O.C.S.O.

Illustrated by William Hart McNichols, S.J.

Our Sunday Visitor Publishing Division
Our Sunday Visitor, Inc.
Huntington, Indiana 46750

Copyright © 1993 by Our Sunday Visitor Publishing
Division
Our Sunday Visitor, Inc.
ALL RIGHTS RESERVED

The English translation of the Scripture texts is taken from the *New Jerusalem Bible*, Doubleday, ©1987 except in those instances where it is the author's own translation from the original languages.

With the exception of short excerpts for critical reviews, no part of this book may be reproduced or transmitted in any form or by any means, electronic or mechanical, including photocopying, recording, or by any information storage or retrieval system, without permission in writing from the publisher. Write:
Our Sunday Visitor Publishing Division
Our Sunday Visitor, Inc.
200 Noll Plaza
Huntington, Indiana 46750

ISBN: 0-87973-499-X
LCCCN: 92-61553

PRINTED IN THE UNITED STATES OF AMERICA

Cover design by Monica Watts

499

By the same author

DAILY WE TOUCH HIM
Practical Religious Experiences

CENTERING PRAYER
Renewing an Ancient Christian Prayer Form

CENTERED LIVING
The Way of Centering Prayer

O HOLY MOUNTAIN
Journal of a Retreat on Mount Athos

IN SEARCH OF TRUE WISDOM
Visits to Eastern Spiritual Fathers and Mothers

CHALLENGES IN PRAYER

LAST OF THE FATHERS

BREAKING BREAD
The Table Talk of Jesus

A MANUAL OF LIFE
The New Testament for Daily Reading

MARY TODAY
Challenging Woman, Model for Maturing Christians

THOMAS MERTON, BROTHER MONK
The Quest for True Freedom

DAILY WE FOLLOW HIM
Learning Discipleship from Peter

THE MONASTIC WAY

PRAYERTIMES: MORNING — MIDDAY — EVENING
A Pocket "Liturgy of the Hours" for All Christians

A RETREAT WITH THOMAS MERTON

LIVING OUR PRIESTHOOD TODAY

THROUGH THE YEAR WITH THE SAINTS
A Daily Companion for Private or Liturgical Prayer

LONG ON THE JOURNEY
The Reflections of a Pilgrim

LIGHT FROM THE CLOISTER

PRAYING BY HAND

Contents

Foreword	7
Introduction	9
The Five Joyful Mysteries	19
The Annunciation	21
The Visitation	29
The Birth of Jesus	41
The Presentation of Jesus in the Temple	51
The Finding of Jesus in the Temple	61
The Five Sorrowful Mysteries	69
Agony and Consolation	71
Jesus Is Scourged	79
Jesus Is Crowned with Thorns	87
Jesus Carries His Cross	97
The Crucifixion	107
The Five Glorious Mysteries	117
The Resurrection	119
The Ascension	127
The Descent of the Holy Spirit upon the Apostles	135

The Assumption of the Blessed Virgin Mary 145

The Coronation of the Blessed Virgin Mary 155

The Prayers of the Rosary 163

Foreword

This is a rather unique volume. It comes out of a friendship, out of the prayer and love of two friends. Two men, quite unalike, and yet alike in many ways, too. Both are men who belong to God, consecrated to him by vows; men who have decided that Christ-God will be the empowering central love of their lives; they have heard an invitation and in their own faltering ways have responded. They both have been graced, unworthy though they be, by a share in Christ's ministerial priesthood. They have some common friends, in heaven — like Saint Aloysius — and on earth — like the PWAs (Persons with AIDS) they have loved and served. One is younger, the other older. One uses his pen and pencil, and brush, too, to create line and image, color and form. The other uses pen and pencil, and a word processor, too, to form sentences and paragraphs, chapters and bibliographies. They both lay out on the page images and symbols which they hope in some way share what they have seen within and open the way for you to enter into the same experience and move beyond it to still richer and fuller experiences of the All Pervasive Love.

There has been a special joy in creating this book, a joy that comes from working with someone you love. We have worked with our Divine Lover, trying to let him guide us all the way. We hope we have not missed too many of his leadings. And we have worked with our Mother. It is her rosary; it is her book. As children, we happily give it to our mother. And we have worked together, knowing the frustration of miles of separation and the distraction of many other projects, but happy to have this project to weave our lives together. May it please our Lord and our Lady.

Father M. Basil Pennington, O.C.S.O.
Feast of the Holy Rosary

Introduction

The rosary! It is amazing how powerfully a little chain of beads can enter into our lives.

Perhaps you can remember when you received your first rosary. Was it at First Communion? At the end of Mass we opened our First Communion packet with its prayer book, scapular, medals, and rosary, and we proudly held up our beads while Father called down upon them the different blessings that promise various indulgences when we prayed the rosary as we ought. Or maybe the rosary came into your hands much earlier as you joined in the daily family rosary in your home. Or did you have to find it on your own? Perhaps you are a convert and discovered this 'Catholic thing' only later in life. In any case, the rosary is ours now and it is a powerful presence in our lives.

Even if there have been periods when it hung,

apparently idle, on our bed post or sat in a dresser drawer, or when it was carried, seemingly unused, in pocket or purse, the rosary was not idle or unused. It was a present to us as a presence. A chain binding us to heaven and the Queen of heaven. It spoke of divine hope and love. In our busyness we rarely stopped to listen to its message in any reflective way. But it was there and it was good to have it there. We kept the rosary in our lives and it spoke to our lives.

One of the reasons why the rosary does sometimes become a less used presence in our lives is because of the difficulty we experience in using it in a meaningful way. Even those of us who, perhaps out of a sense of duty or loyalty to Mary and the Church, have daily fingered the beads, still we have at times found them less than eloquent. The fact is, though, the rosary brings to us a word of life, a message that has of itself ever-renewed depths of meaning. Each day, and many times a day if we will but listen, the rosary is ready to speak to us of love, a love beyond all expressions of hope, a hope that wins out beyond the apparently ultimate defeat of the grave, yes, beyond even nuclear holocaust.

It can be very helpful to us in our desire to have the rosary in our lives as a daily meaningful and enriching encounter with Jesus and Mary, with our God of love, if we are familiar with various ways to pray the rosary and alternately make use of them. This variety not only offsets tedium but speaks to various levels of our being, satisfying even as it challenges them.

The simplest, if not the easiest way, to pray the beads, is to pray the prayers of the rosary. As it was often expressed by the Fathers of the Church, we let our mind and heart be one with our lips. We deliberately profess our faith: *I believe in God . . . and in Jesus Christ . . . I believe in the Holy Spirit. . . .* We pray to the Father the *Our Father*, the prayer that Jesus taught us. We join the angel in saying, again and again, *Hail, Mary. . . .* We prostrate in our hearts: *Glory be to the Father and to the Son and to the Holy Spirit. . . .* This is a very simple way to pray — but not an easy one. Our minds tend to wander. Repetition tends to numb us. We may fall asleep. In fact, this is a good way to pray when we do want to go to sleep.

There are tremendous depths of meaning in these simple prayers. Saints have written whole books on the *Our Father*. As our simple repetition becomes more reflective, these depths begin to reveal themselves to us. The messages touch our lives and become alive in us. If ever we come to realize fully what it means to call God, in truth, our Father, our lives will indeed be transformed.

There will, then, be times in all our lives when we can fruitfully pray the rosary in this way. We should not look down upon this way: It is *only* vocal prayer. The important thing is *prayer*, to be consciously in communion with our God of love. And usually, the simpler our activity in opening to this communion, the more space God has to commune with us, effectively revealing his very special love for us. "Unless you be as a little child, you cannot enter the Kingdom of Heaven." Like little ones, we unabashedly welcome all the love with which our heavenly Father* wishes to embrace us.

Inevitably as we pray with our fingers and our lips, our minds and our hearts must come into the prayer. They at least set the fingers and lips into motion. Then what do they do? As we have seen, our minds and our hearts can seek to come into accord with the words our lips are forming. Or they may attend to God in some other way.

Very early in the development of the rosary, events from the revelation were associated with the praying of the beads. "Faith comes through hearing." Hearing, at least interiorly, these words of Scripture as we pray the beads enlivens our faith and gives direction to our hope and love. Eloquent teachers found an appropriate sentence of Scripture to go with each bead. This way of praying the rosary has seen a renaissance in recent years. It has been called the scriptural rosary. Books are available offering the texts to be said or reflected upon as each bead passes through our fingers.

In earlier days, before the advent of inexpensive printing and widespread literacy, the task of remembering all these texts was too daunting for many a person. Others found it all too much. Something simpler was desired. Soon enough, fifteen basic events in the lives of Jesus and Mary were commonly chosen as the objects for the mind to meditate upon. The American bishops have reminded us that we need not restrict ourselves to the fifteen particular mysteries which have become traditional in the course of the last few centuries. Nonetheless these fifteen do cover well the journey of Jesus and Mary, inviting us to enter into the most significant moments of their lives, the moments that wrought and modeled our salvation.

There are different ways in which we can approach these mysteries. We can preface each decade with a short reading from the pertinent Scriptures. If we are accustomed to pray the rosary frequently, these passages may be fully present to us, engraved in our memories. But when we allow the Lord to speak to us through the inspired words, he has a way of giving familiar words new meaning as he speaks to us where we are today — here and now. A wide open listening invites the Lord to expand our minds and hearts and then fill the new space with the message of his love — a message too big for any space, a message that always has more to say to us. This message can then abide with us as we pray the decades and allow the message to sink deeper and deeper into us. It can form our hearts and call forth a renewed heartfelt prayer.

Perhaps the most common way in which we meditate on the mysteries during the recitation of the rosary is to use the imagination. We picture for ourselves a scene portraying the sacred event. Here, too, an enriching variety is possible. One day, we might stand outside the scene, looking in, following all the action, listening to the participants. We let the unfolding sacred history speak to us, pausing on one facet or another. Or we might note how a particular virtue, one we need in our own lives, is coming to play in the event. For example, in the first sorrowful mystery, Jesus' great compassion, highlighted by Peter's lack of it, is apparent. Our imagination, guided we hope by the Holy Spirit, fills in the spaces left by the Scriptures. Other days we might enter the scene and identify with one or another of the participants: with Jesus, with Mary (How did she see these happenings?), with the angels, with the crowds, the ordinary people, the leaders, the different apostles, and so on. In the Spirit, there can be a deep faith sharing here.

Perhaps though, we have seen enough, heard enough, thought enough, said enough — at least for now — and we just want to be quiet for a bit, resting in the mystery, in the love it bespeaks. The simple but powerful drawings of Father McNichols found in this volume can invite us to do just that. As so many "icons," as we pray each decade we can just let our eyes attentively rest in the eyes and faces portrayed here. That will say enough. It can say it all. Nothing more need be said. The fullness of love is present to us and we are completely present to it — as completely a "yes" as we are capable of being.

There are many ways in which you might use this volume as an aid in praying the rosary. Do feel free to use it in any way that is useful to you. I offer a few suggestions here in the hope of being somewhat helpful.

At *first*, you might want to ignore the meditations of the author and just *use the pictures*. You might set the book before you as you pray your rosary, gazing gently on the respective picture as you pray through the decades. Let the picture draw you out and invite you in. Look into the eyes and go through them into the inner depths of the experience. Let the Spirit lead you into the hidden places of reality. Thoughts are not needed. We do not need to articulate the reality. We want to just let it be and let it be in us. Let it call us into our own full participation in the divine action. Let the mysteries, as mysteries, come to be within. You may never want to do anything else with this volume but this. So be it. You have chosen the better part, and let no one take it from you.

But some days you may feel the need for some help to enter in. You might try a second method. As the book lies quietly there before you, *let the words of the Sacred Text begin to speak to you*. Never feel obligated to push on. If the first words speak deeply to you, rest with them as you pray the decade. The rest of the words will be there for some other day. We have no need to finish them all. We have all eternity for that. Take each day the *manna*, the words, that will feed, and leave the rest.

Some days though, the words themselves may also seem silent. We let them all speak to us, but they seem to say nothing. They are familiar sounds, with grammatical sense, but no effective message of life. On such days we might try a *third* method. When all the words lay there like an array of dead letters, *choose a few or even one and carry it with you as you pray the decade*. Let the chosen word or phrase quietly repeat itself within your heart as you pray the *Aves*, and perhaps before you finish the ten, your chosen "word" will have come alive and you will have much reason to say: Glory be to the Father and to the Son and to the Holy Spirit. In any case, another of the words of God is engraved in your heart as a sure defense, a word of life.

Only after you have given the enlivening Spirit ample opportunity to speak to you through Father McNichols' inspiring renditions of the pictures of our tradition and through Spirit's own inspired words, will you want to move on to the words that the Spirit has given through inspiring the author of the meditations. Here again, no rush. No need to read on and on. Take a little bit, a sentence or two, or a paragraph, and chew it through the decade.

This does not mean you can not at some point take time out and read through a whole chapter or the entire book. This might be good, putting everything in context. But at the time of prayer, when you are actually using the volume while you are praying your beads, do not let your mind get all caught up in the fascination of ideas and images. Prayer is the thing, communion and union with God.

---

*I am conscious of the fact that some are not comfortable with using exclusively masculine nouns and pronouns for referring to God. I feel with these sisters and brothers. They are very right in their insight that in fact God is neither male nor female — the fullness of the qualities of both are in our God. Yet I find that using the personal nomination of Father has warmth, depth and meaning for me that is lacking in the more neutral "parent." And I have to confess, that speaking of God as "mother" is still a bit artificial for me, and, I believe, for many others. I am accustomed to hearing Jesus refer to God as Father, and I identify deeply with Jesus. I believe then my sharing with you is more authentic at this time if I speak of the First Person of the Blessed Trinity as Father. I will rely on your kindness to hear this with graciousness and to let it be heard in your life in the way it is most fruitful for you.

I would add, if I may: We do have a real need to get in touch with the maternal aspects of God (but let us not get sexist ourselves in denominating various qualities as male or female). At the same time we need to take care not to lose the strong masculine and fatherly presence of God in our lives. We are seeing not only 'a generation without fathers' but generations with an obliteration or confusion of gender roles — a great human impoverishment. God has given us Mary as mother so that he can be more powerfully present to us as he was to Jesus, the Son into whom we are baptized, in his fatherly role.

The Five Joyful Mysteries

The First Joyful Mystery:
The Annunciation

In the sixth month the angel Gabriel was sent by God to a town in Galilee called Nazareth to a virgin betrothed to a man named Joseph, of the House of David; and the virgin's name was Mary. He went in and said to her, "Rejoice, you who enjoy God's favor! The Lord is with you." She was deeply disturbed by these words and asked herself what this greeting could mean, but the angel said to her, "Mary, do not be afraid; you have won God's favor. Look! You are to conceive in your womb and bear a son, and you must name him Jesus. He will be great and will be called Son of the Most High. The Lord God will give him the throne of his ancestor David; he will rule over the House of Jacob for ever and his reign will have no end." Mary said to the angel, "But how can this come about, since I have no knowledge of man?" The angel answered, "The Holy Spirit will come upon you and the power of the Most High will cover you with its shadow. And so the child will be holy and will be called Son of God. And I tell you this too; your cousin Elizabeth also, in her old age, has conceived a son and she whom people called barren is now in her sixth month, for nothing is impossible to God." Mary said, "You see before you the Lord's servant, let it happen to me as you have said." And the angel left her.

— Luke 1:26-38

Archangel Gabriel
from Orazio Gentileschi (c. 1563, Pisa — c. 1647,
England), "Annunciation" (1623), painted in Genoa,
now in the Galleria Sabaudi, Turin, Italy.

The Annunciation

An angel!

It does not quite fit in our everyday sort of things. In fact, we have to invest him/her with some sort of human form.

Mary was familiar enough with angels, or at least with the idea of angels. She had been nurtured on the Scriptures. And the Scriptures are full of angels. The Scriptures are not too descriptive in presenting them. They evidently did take on some sort of human form. Three — were they angels or the Trinity itself? — came to Abraham and Sarah to announce another miraculous birth. Unbeknownst to Mary, only a few months before one of the heavenly messengers stood at the right hand of the altar of incense in the temple at Jerusalem and told Zechariah of another miraculous conception — like Abraham and Sarah's, a miracle of old age, yet one intimately connected with this very young virgin.

The angel points to what is above, beyond all our everyday experience; indeed, beyond what our poor minds can fully grasp, to most sublime mystery, to what eye has not seen nor ear heard, nor has it even entered into the human mind.

Mary had grown up within and been fully formed by a people who had been able to keep their proper sense as a unique and chosen people because they cherished the precious revelation that God is one and unique, Yahweh. There is no God but our God. Listen, O Israel, your God is one God, the only true God.

Now, suddenly, not only is Mary confronted with the appearance of an angel — as frightening, awesome, and troublesome as that might be — but this angel tells her Yahweh has a son. And what is more, she is to be the mother of that son. What is a twelve-year-old Jewish girl to do with that?

Mary had already matured much. She had gone through a very extraordinary and graced discernment. And she had drawn another into it, the man she was betrothed to marry. Despite the Lord's command to increase and multiply and the universal Jewish response to that command, Mary had discerned a unique call to live in a virginal marriage. Was she all wrong? She only wanted to do God's will.

But this was not a question of an ordinary

maternity. The angel pointed to something unfathomably sublime. A divine pregnancy. A virginal pregnancy. Didn't this belong to the mythology of the pagans who conquered and sought to seduce the Jews? This was real. Grace abounded in this encounter. There was no doubt in the authenticity of this message and messenger. Only the inconceivability of a divine conceiving.

Mary had no concepts, no images, which could embrace the reality that was being revealed to her. She could only give herself, follow the direction of the angel, and let mystery descend upon her and expand her whole being, filling it with the divine at every level of being. Her only answer could be: "Let it happen to me" — a totally active passivity. A being that said a complete and unbounded "yes" to God, to let the divine bring forth the inconceivable within her through a divine conception.

Like Mary we can only allow the fullness of the mystery abide with us, letting it form us, raising us to a new, unheard of, inconceivable sublimity.

For in the Incarnation, not only does God become man — human, but the human, a man becomes God. And all humanity is summoned to divinity. The angel points for us, too, to what is beyond, above, beyond everything we can conceive. God became man in order that man — and woman — might become divine — true partakers of the divine nature and life. What can we do with this inconceivable concept?

Like Mary, we can only say our own *Fiat*. Let it happen to me according to your word, your plan, your will.

The angel, with all the dynamism of her being, invites us to go beyond. Word and gesture, eye and finger invite us to transcend. No thoughts are too sublime for us — if only we remember it is a divine invitation. It is all gift. Ours is but to receive. To wholly receive, to put no limits on our receiving, to hang on to none of our own limitations. To let God be God in us and bring us into a whole new level of being. Let it happen to me.

Our Father. . . .

The Second Joyful Mystery:
The Visitation

Mary set out at that time and went as quickly as she could into the hill country to a town in Judah. She went into Zechariah's house and greeted Elizabeth. Now it happened that as soon as Elizabeth heard Mary's greeting, the child leapt in her womb and Elizabeth was filled with the Holy Spirit. She gave a loud cry and said, "Of all women you are the most blessed and blessed is the fruit of your womb. Why should I be honored with a visit from the mother of my Lord? Look, the moment your greeting reached my ears, the child in my womb leapt for joy. Yes, blessed is she who believed that the promise made her by the Lord would be fulfilled."
And Mary said:

*My soul proclaims the greatness of the Lord
and my spirit rejoices in God my Savior;
because he has looked upon the humiliation of his servant.
Yes, from now onwards all generations will call me blessed,
for the Almighty has done great things for me.
Holy is his name,
and his faithful love extends age after age to those who fear him.
He has used the power of his arm,
he has routed the arrogant of heart.
He has pulled down princes from their thrones and raised high the lowly.
He has filled the starving with good things, sent the rich away empty.*

He has come to the help of Israel his servant, mindful of his faithful love
— according to the promise he made to our ancestors
— of his mercy to Abraham and to his descendants for ever.

Mary stayed with her some three months and then went home.
— Luke 1:39-56

Mary and Elizabeth from Pontormo (Jacopo Carucci) (1494, Pontormo — 1557, Florence), "The Visitation" (1513), Porch of the Church of the Annunciation, Florence.

The Visitation

Mary — she was like a beautiful cup of the finest gold, a ciborium set with the most precious stones and covered with a silken veil, hidden in the tabernacle and brought out only to bring the Eucharistic Lord to others. Mary's life was so completely hidden.

We know little about it. When and where was she born? Who were her parents? The apocrypha tell delightful tales of her being presented in the temple at Jerusalem when she was three. She danced on the steps of the Holy of Holies and gave joy to every heart. From that time she grew up within the sanctuary close to the holy place. Such fanciful things were hardly possible, though the site of Saint Anne's Church, which is said to cover her home, is very close to the temple precincts.

How her virginal marriage with Joseph, the

just man from Nazareth, was arranged is also unknown to us. We only know she was betrothed to him and living in Nazareth when the angel came to ask her to be the mother of God. She heard the message with an enlightened faith and said her wholehearted "yes."

The angel had told her of another special pregnancy, that of her aged cousin Elizabeth. It was not exactly meant to be a sign to Mary. Her faith did not need signs. It was more a word of comfort. And a call to comfort and assist the elderly woman in her hour.

With great courage Mary made the journey south. It took a lot of courage. What explanation did she give to her parents or guardians and to her espoused? She undoubtedly joined a pilgrim band or a merchant caravan that was heading for Jerusalem. The group probably did not dare to set out directly through alien Samaritan territory. The journey down along the river would be safer, but certainly longer and hotter. It would be a difficult journey for a young woman who was entering into the mystery of her first pregnancy and would not have any female confidant at her side to support her. All the while she must have wondered how things would be worked out with Joseph and her family. The future was full of awesome and fearful questions.

As she entered the courtyard of Zechariah's

home, there was the elderly woman so obviously pregnant. Mary's cry of love reached receptive ears. Elizabeth all but leapt up herself, her face aglow:

> *Of all women you are the most blessed and blessed is the fruit of your womb. Why should I be honored with a visit from the mother of my Lord? Look, the moment your greeting reached my ears, the child in my womb leapt for joy. Yes, blessed is she who believed that the promise made her by the Lord would be fulfilled.*

Yes, Elizabeth knew. And Mary's mission had begun.

Elizabeth knew. There was another with whom Mary could share her sublime secret. And all her fears and wonderment in their pregnancies. What days and weeks these two cousins must have had together. Even in that first moment of encounter, as they rushed into each other's arms, Mary could feel her Son's cousin dancing for joy within his mother. The kick of life told her so much of what was to be. In how many ways was Elizabeth to assure her, enable her to foresee what was to come, help her to confidently trust that her Son's Father would resolve all the difficulties with Joseph and the family.

And Mary's mission had begun. The mission which Mary would henceforth exercise, most times in hidden ways. She would be bringing

Jesus, the Savior, her Son and God's, to others — bringing his outpouring grace, his prophetic insight, his abounding joy. Mary had begun that mission which we speak of as we hail her as the mediatrix of all grace. At Cana we will get a glimpse of her active mediation. On Calvary we will see her intimate association with her Son and hear the divine command that she is to mother all of us, the whole Christ. As Pentecost approaches, a fearful Church will be gathered around her in prayer. But for the most part hers will be a hidden service, a quiet ministry of prayer and love. It is only in these very first days of her ministry that God gives us a clear intimation as to what Mary's role is to be in the plan of salvation. She is to bring to each one of us our Savior with all his grace and joy.

We can understand Mary's role in our lives most fully, I think, if we envision our lives as being lived in the womb, in preparation to being born to eternal life. Christian tradition has always called the day of death the *dies natalis*, the day of birth, the day we are born to unending life. During the long gestation of this temporal life, which may well last nine decades, though probably less, Mary is mothering, nurturing, constantly channeling to us a participation in divine life and all that sustains such life in us. Through her ministry as through a life cord, the graces are coming to us that will enable us to grow into a full Christ-person. Mary brings us Christ, our true joy, the source of all our life and hope. With this presence, even though we do not see and still live in faith in the darkness of the womb, we can, like John, leap and dance for joy.

Our Father. . . .

The Third Joyful Mystery:
The Birth of Jesus

Now it happened that at this time Caesar Augustus issued a decree that a census should be made of the whole inhabited world. This census — the first — took place while Quirinius was governor of Syria and everyone went to be registered, each to his own town. So Joseph set out from the town of Nazareth in Galilee for Judaea, to David's town called Bethlehem, since he was of David's house and line, in order to be registered with Mary, his betrothed, who was with child. Now it happened that, while they were there, the time came for her to have her child and she gave birth to a son, her first-born. She wrapped him in swaddling clothes and laid him in a manger because there was no room for them in the living-space.

In the countryside close by there were shepherds out in the fields keeping guard over their sheep during the watches of the night. An angel of the Lord stood over them and the glory of the Lord shone round them. They were terrified but the angel said, "Do not be afraid. Look, I bring you news of great joy, a joy to be shared by the whole people. Today in the town of David a Savior has been born to you; he is Christ the Lord. And here is a sign for you: you will find a baby wrapped in swaddling clothes and laying in a manger." And all at once with the angel there was a great throng of the hosts of heaven, praising God with the words:

> *Glory to God in the highest heaven,*
> *and on earth peace for those he favors.*

Now it happened that when the angels had gone from them into heaven, the shepherds said to one another, "Let us go to Bethlehem and see this event which the Lord has made known to us." So they hurried away and found Mary and Joseph and the baby lying in the manger. When they saw the child they repeated what they had been told about him and everyone who heard it was astonished at what the shepherds said to them. As for Mary, she treasured all these things and pondered them in her heart. And the shepherds went back glorifying and praising God for all they had heard and seen, just as they had been told.
— Luke 2:1-20

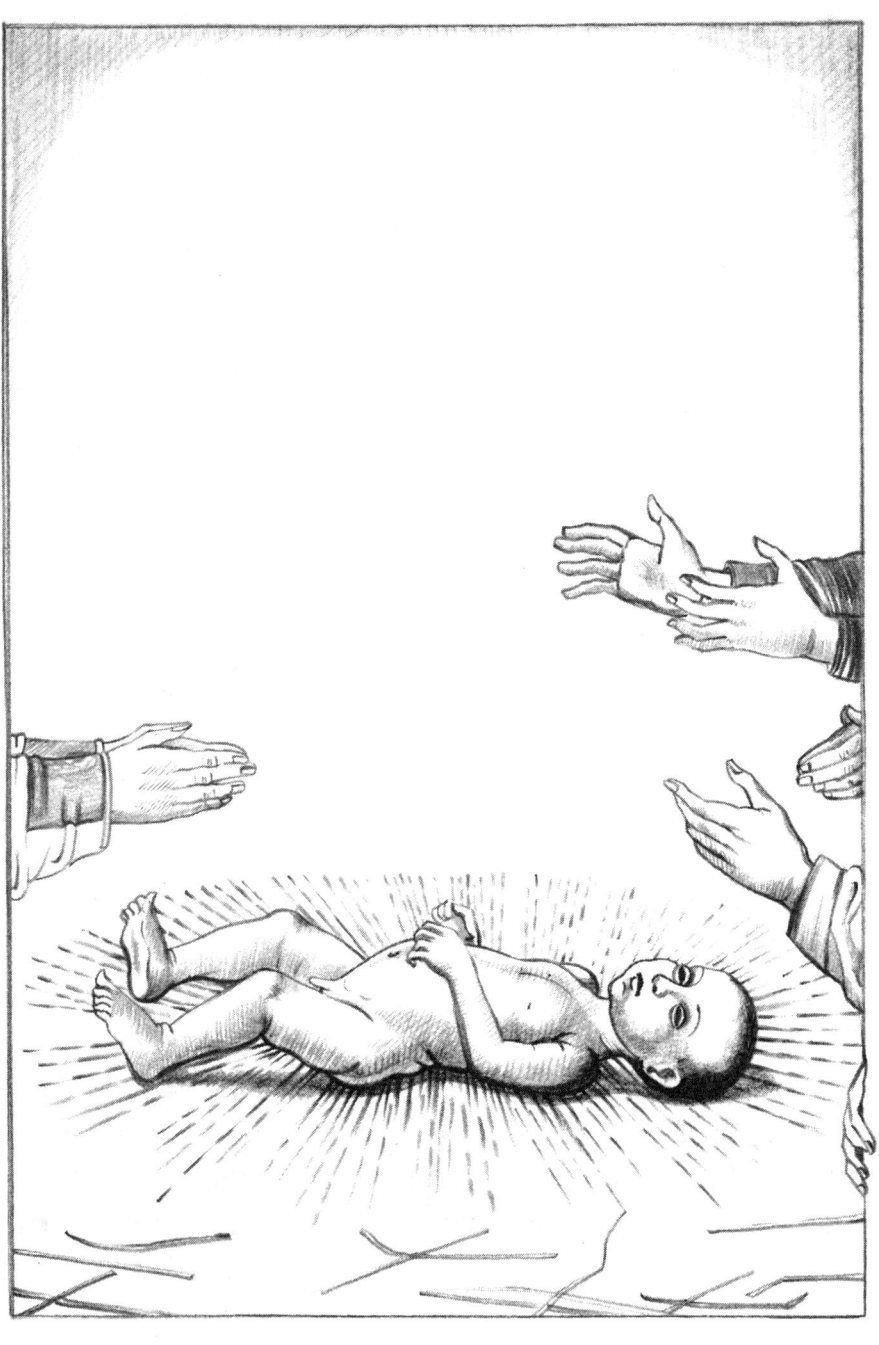

The Newborn Christ
from Hugo van der Goes (c. 1440, Belgium [?] —
1482, Roode Kloister near Brussels, Belgium),
"The Adoration of the Shepherds" (c. 1474-76),
center panel of the Portinari Altarpiece, now in the
Uffizi, Florence.

The Birth of Jesus

How could the Divine enter more completely and more nakedly into the human experience?

Quickly, the swaddling clothes, those so carefully prepared by Mary, hide his nakedness, protect his vulnerability. Who wants a God so vulnerable, so human, so needy?

He became like us in all things but sin.

Hands through the centuries reach out to him. We need, in our weakness, sin, and misery, a God who is compassionately vulnerable.

Can a God so vulnerable not be compassionate with our weakness? Indeed it is our weakness that he has taken on to be so vulnerable.

He lies there, almost like an abortion. A life cast out of the warm embracing sanctuary of the womb. The divine is cast upon our earth, clothing himself with all our earthliness.

We sometimes need to be shocked by seeing

the penis of God. We are all too prone to leave God out of whole areas of our life. But he wants in. He became — fully, freely, because he wanted it — one with us in our humanity. And every detail of it. He did not sin. But he embraced our sin and carried it with his sinless and totally vulnerable body to the nakedness of the cross. Again, people saw the penis of God as he hung there, hiding nothing of his humanity, crucified, in agony, because we in so many ways fail to accept the fullness of our humanity. And all too often live more like animals than integrated humans.

Naked he came forth from the womb. In the womb of Mary he knew the embrace of a love worthy of him. He left the embrace — as painful as was the separation for him and for her — to be here for us.

How can even the most despised of sinners fear to approach a tiny newborn?

He came for us and for our salvation. He wants to be totally available to us, totally accessible. With all the attractive neediness of a tiny one, he lies there inviting our love and care.

Yet there is something about this Newborn that causes our outreaching hands to fold in prayer. For us and for our salvation he is here.

He speaks to us, too, of the sacredness of all life. If all the fullness of the Godhead can be present to us corporally in this littlest bit of humanity, then how can any least bit of humanity not be most sacred? The poor eyes with which we fail to see — to see the divine beauty hidden in every human. How easily are we deceived, blinded by color, shape, what we call deformity, disease. This little Jewish child, one more to be counted in the hated census of the august Romans. This child is our God!

Come, let us adore.

And let our eyes be opened, our vision perfected. Let us see the divine in every child, in the womb or out, in every human. And let us reverence.

Let us reach out, to give the support that is needed, to get the support we need. Human solidarity took on a new dimension when God became one of us. There is nothing of humanity that is not divinized — nothing of the divine that does not now belong to us, to each one of us. Hence the sacredness of all human life — because God did become man — human. He came forth from the womb of a woman — of a human. And presented himself to us as a vulnerable little human with hands and heart and a penis that would know the knife of circumcision. Behold, here is our God. If only we can be shocked enough to truly adore.

Our Father. . . .

The Fourth Joyful Mystery:
The Presentation of Jesus in the Temple

And when the day came for Jesus and Mary to be purified in keeping with the law of Moses, Mary and Joseph took him up to Jerusalem to present him to the Lord — observing what is written in the Law of the Lord: Every first-born male must be consecrated to the Lord — and also to offer in sacrifice, in accordance with what is prescribed in the Law of the Lord, a pair of turtledoves or two young pigeons. Now in Jerusalem there was a man named Simeon. He was an upright and devout man; he looked forward to the restoration of Israel and the Holy Spirit rested on him. It had been revealed to him by the Holy Spirit that he would not see death until he had set eyes on the Christ of the Lord. Prompted by the Spirit he came to the Temple and when the parents brought in the child Jesus to do for him what the Law required, he took him into his arms and blessed God and he said:

Now, Master, you are letting your servant go in peace as you promised;
for my eyes have seen the salvation
which you have made ready in the sight of the nations;
a light of revelation for the gentiles
and glory for your people Israel.

As the child's father and mother were wondering at the things that were being said about him, Simeon blessed them and said to Mary his mother, "Look, he is destined for the fall and the rise of many in Israel, destined to be a sign that is opposed — and a sword will pierce your soul, too — so that the secret thoughts of many may be laid bare."

There was a prophetess, too, Anna the daughter of Phanuel, of the tribe of Asher. She was well on in years. Her days of girlhood over, she had been married for seven years before becoming a widow. She was now eighty-four years old and never left the Temple, serving God night and day with fasting and prayer. She came up just at that moment and began to praise God; and she spoke of the child to all who looked forward to the deliverance of Jerusalem.

— Luke 2:22-38

Simeon and Anna with Jesus
from Jan Provost II (c. 1465, Mons — 1529, Bruges),
"The Presentation."

The Presentation of Jesus in the Temple

Mary holds her Child a bit more tightly. She holds him close to her breast. There is a certain foreboding. Why?

Perhaps it is because this is the temple, the house of his Father. And she is made all too aware of other claims that can be made on her Son. *Every firstborn shall be called holy to the Lord.*

Perhaps it is the two little pigeons that are to be offered in sacrifice. There is something fearful about sacrifice: the destruction of life, innocent life, the just for the unjust. Mary is happy that her husband has not disappeared into the Court of the Israelites with the minister who takes their offering to the priests. (This most holy of all God's creatures, this woman is not considered worthy to enter into the inner precincts of this holy place — just because she is a woman.) His warm, strong arm is most comforting.

Perhaps it is Simeon who now approaches

them. There is a deep joy in his face, a serenity, a peace. But when she looks into his eyes, Mary sees something else. Looking into those eyes the young mother experiences a great reluctance to place her Little One into his outstretched arms. Men can be so clumsy in handling such fragility.

Yet she cannot refuse.

He does indeed hold her Little One with much gentle loving care. Yet his eyes are not on the Little One. They are on her. The prophetic words pour forth: *Now, Master, . . . my eyes have seen the salvation which you have made ready in the sight of the nations; a light of revelation for the gentiles and glory for your people Israel.* And then those words that do exactly what they speak of: *Look, he is destined for the fall and the rise of many in Israel, destined to be a sign that is opposed — and a sword will pierce your soul, too. . . .*

The sword plunges deep into the heart of the young mother. What should be a most happy moment for this young couple is marred. All Mary's foreboding seems to be realized. This visit to the temple, to his Father's house, affirms the higher claims upon him. He is to be the savior of his people, as the angel had foretold. And salvation comes through sacrifice. The drops of blood poured out upon the altar from the little pigeons foretell another outpouring of blood that Mary would rather not envision at this moment — or ever.

Many years later the day would come when Mary would approach her Son and he would take it as the occasion to give an important teaching — a teaching begun with a question as is the rabbinical way: *Who is . . . my mother? Everyone who does the will of my Father in heaven is . . . mother to me.*

Christ has been conceived in each of us at baptism. And we are called to mother the Christ-nature within us.

We bring him to the temple that is within. And we know our own foreboding as we come to the gates of the sanctuary, and reason and imagination which are usually so much in charge of everything, are asked to let go and we are invited to enter into the deeper, apparently dark regions of the contemplative communion of Christ with his Father. We fear what it might mean: the sacrifice of all that we have come to be identified with as the false self. It is hard to let go. We cherish the Christ within us. But if we do not let go he cannot be about his Father's business — bringing us to full participation in the Christ life. He will be restricted to *our* business.

We have our reluctance, our fear, too, in entrusting this Christlife of ours to the hands of the priests — the doddering old priests who seem so inept, the careless priests who do not seem to be sensitive to all our concerns, the priests who call to a sacrifice and a mission that seem to be beyond us. Yet without church and sacrament we cannot enter fully into the all-redeeming sacrifice of the Christ whom we are called to be.

And what of that other pair of eyes upon us, the eyes of Anna? Mary's own mother had been an Anna. There was something of motherly tenderness and compassion present in this holy old woman in this hour when the young mother heard the words of dire prophecy already being fulfilled: . . . *and a sword will pierce your own heart.* His mission, the mission of her Son, is glorious, hope is renewed, but a sword does indeed pierce the all-too-knowing heart of the young mother.

What for all the people, for all of us, is a sign of great joy — the coming of our Savior, the all-saving sacrifice, into the temple of the Father — has its cost. And that cost cut deeply into the heart of this beautiful young mother. A day of purest joy and promise, the coming of the Savior into his temple, the beginning of the work of salvation is not without its birth pains. As long as we are on the journey through this vale of tears, joy and pain are not far apart. This is a joyful mystery, for he has come for us and for our salvation. But it has its pain written deep within for the cost of our salvation is his crucifixion. And we who have been baptized into Christ must share in that pain.

Our Father. . . .

The Fifth Joyful Mystery:

The Finding of Jesus in the Temple

Every year Jesus' parents used to go to Jerusalem for the feast of the Passover. When he was twelve years old, they went up for the feast as usual. When the days of the feast were over and they set off for home, the boy Jesus stayed behind in Jerusalem without his parents knowing it. They assumed he was somewhere in the party and it was only after a day's journey that they went to look for him among their relations and acquaintances. When they failed to find him they went back to Jerusalem looking for him everywhere.

It happened that, three days later, they found him in the Temple, sitting among the teachers, listening to them and asking them questions; and all those who heard him were astounded at his intelligence and his replies. They were overcome when they saw him and his mother said to him, "My child, why have you done this to us? See how worried your father and I have been, looking for you." He replied, "Why were you looking for me? Did you not know that I must be in my father's house?" But they did not understand what he meant.

He went down with them and came to Nazareth and lived under their authority. His mother stored up all these things in her heart. And Jesus increased in wisdom, in stature and in favor with God and with people.

— Luke 2:41-52

Jesus, Mary, and Joseph
from William Holman Hunt (1827-1910, London),
"The Finding in the Temple" (1860), now in the
Birmingham Gallery.

The Finding of Jesus in the Temple

He is just a boy.

Yet we had better say, a young man. He is twelve. He has made his bar mitzvah. Before the law he is now a man, with all the privileges — and obligations of a son of Abraham, a man among the people of God. That is why he accompanied Joseph and Mary on the long pilgrimage to Jerusalem, skirting alien country, knowing the burning sun of the desert road.

Yet he is still Mary's little boy. He always will be. But a searing school of detachment will assert another reality. In his divine wisdom the Child decided it is time to begin these harsh lessons.

The emotions are high here, many and mixed. Mary's anguished heart knows a great relief. She clings to her child. She presses her face against his. She wants not only to touch him, but to smell him. She would taste him, if she could. The deepest human instincts of a mother are at play here.

Her relief is great, but her anguish, so powerfully present for three days, must have its outlet. "Son, why? Why have you done this — done this to me — and to your father?"

What thoughts possessed the mind of this inward man?

It had been almost twelve years since he accompanied her to this temple. Together, in ritual offering they acknowledged this child belonged to God. Of all the firstborn he was the Firstborn — the Son of the Most High, the angel had said. This reality remained perhaps more present to Joseph as he reflectively went about his daily life. Though he trained the young hands to the carpenter's tasks, I do not think he ever forgot that this Little One who called him *"abba"* was not in truth his son. This fact in no way lessened his anguish these past few days. The paternity he shared was necessarily mysterious. If anything it demanded of him a love and care beyond that of any mortal fatherhood. In the reunion and in the dialogue that ensued he could only wonder, marvel, experience more profoundly that attitude we call humility.

Mary, as true mother, and perhaps even more

enlightened than Joseph in regard to the real nature of her Son, with a profound joy and deep realization had brought their Son to his Father, fully acknowledging that this firstborn is his Firstborn. But as the weeks and months and years went by and she enjoyed all the intimacies and services of a mother toward her little one, it was very easy to forget that there was another dimension to this son of hers. He was so like every other little boy — *like us in all things but sin.* Yes, at the presentation Mary had wholeheartedly given her Son to his Father. Yet, she was not prepared for the Father to so suddenly take him, for her Twelve-Year-Old to suddenly leave the long-accepted pattern and be about his Father's business, remaining in his Father's house?

How often in moments of fervor have we offered ourselves completely to God? We are all his — to do with us whatever he wants. And then one day — it usually seems quite sudden — he claims what has been offered to him. He steps into our lives with some new claim, perhaps some cross, a new vocation or a shift in the ongoing pattern of our life. Perhaps he seems to have walked out of our lives; he is no longer with us — all too docile to our wills. "Lord, why have you done this to me?"

His answer to us, is as it was to Mary: "Did you not know I must be about my Father's business?"

— that business of helping us become selfless, self-giving saints.

We had best be careful what we say to the Lord in our moments of fervor. He takes us seriously. Fortunately for us, grace moves us to moments of loving folly. We are ready to give all. We offer all. Know well: He will take all. That is what he wants. He'll be satisfied with nothing less. Because he wants to wholly transform us to divine children beatifically happy, filled to overflowing with the divine joy.

If as we pray our beads he seems to be lost to us, be comforted. Seek him as Mary and Joseph, assured that with them we will find him and find that he is about his Father's loving business of making us his saints, his holy, wholly happy ones.

Our Father. . . .

The Five Sorrowful Mysteries

The First Sorrowful Mystery:
Agony and Consolation

Jesus and his disciples came to a plot of land called Gethsemane and he said to his disciples, "Stay here while I pray." Then he took Peter and James and John with him. And he began to feel terror and anguish. And he said to them, "My soul is sorrowful to the point of death. Wait here and stay awake." And going on a little further he threw himself on the ground and prayed that, if it were possible, this hour might pass him by. "Abba, Father!," he said, "For you everything is possible. Take this cup away from me. But let it be as you, not I, would have it." He came back and found them sleeping and he said to Peter. "Simon, are you asleep? Had you not the strength to stay awake one hour? Stay awake and pray not to be put to the test. The spirit is willing enough, but human nature is weak." Again he went away and prayed, saying the same words. And once more he came back and found them sleeping, their eyes were so heavy; and they could find no answer for him. He came back a third time and said to them, "You can sleep on now and have your rest. It is all over. The hour has come. Now the Son of man is to be betrayed into the hands of sinners. Get up! Let us go! My betrayer is not far away."

— Mark 14:32-42

The Agony in the Garden
from Carl Heinrich Bloch (1834-90, Copenhagen).

Agony and Consolation

It wrings our heart, yet comforts: The obviously depleted figure, wrung out by hours of agony, finding rest upon an angelic shoulder, comfort, and consolation.

Much lies ahead: betrayal, arrest, abandonment, brutal treatment, mockery and derision, hours of lonely suffering, abandonment, and death. But in a sense the worst is over. The "yes" has been said. The rest will in some way make sense because of the yes.

It was not an easy "yes." Feelings, emotions, deep human urges fought against it. Death is unnatural. It tears apart body and soul. Suffering, like death, is a consequence of sin. And this is the sinless One. Death and suffering were not his due. Abandonment made them all the worse and betrayal cut deep. Sweat mysteriously turned to blood. The cry rose from deep within: If it be possible . . . let it pass.

All things are possible for God. Why not this? Yes, it is possible to let it pass — but love still asks for it. "Not my will, but yours." Love answers love — giving the supreme witness to love: *Greater love than this no one has than to lay down his life.* ...

The surrender of love brings ministering angels. We humans have failed him. We are so asleep to reality, so often not there. So often our fear turns us into cowards. "Could you not watch one hour with me?" When was the last time we watched — simply watched an hour with him?

Teresa of Jesus, the great mystic of Ávila, said she would begin her prayer by creeping through the garden till she came to the point where she could watch. And she watched. Watching suffering that says: "See how much I love you" makes great demands on us. What other response can there be than a complete "yes?" Yet we are afraid of a complete "yes." It leaves us so vulnerable. The Beloved can do whatever he wants with us. We don't trust that much. We had rather go to sleep, continue on in our half-conscious way. Alas, never knowing the ultimate ecstacy of total love, of the complete yes of love with its total union and communion.

The Father sent a comforting angel. Did the Hero of the agony really need such comfort? Or was the comforter sent for us and for our sake —

to assure us that when we finally have the courage to pass through our own inner agony — dying to the false self — and say our "yes," comfort will be there?

What was the comforting angel like? Did this one take on human form? And allow his robe to be stained with bloody sweat? We know the human touch of comfort is important. But we know something deeper is more important: A love that says, "I am with you." Such love can reach across the miles, the continents, the oceans.

Recently I experienced the dread-filled loneliness of being thousands of miles from all who know and love me, totally surrounded by an alien culture, living under the terror of a powerful, ruthless regime: China. The knowledge that I was held in loving hearts, praying hearts, albeit on the other side of the planet earth, was immensely comforting.

If we are indeed one with Christ through the transformation of baptism, so our sufferings are his even as his are our redemption, and his comforting is ours. The visitations of divine comfort, even if they do not take visible angelic form, are never absent from us in our distress, if we but open ourselves to them in a "yes," to the perhaps mysterious but ever-loving will of the Father. "Not my will but yours be done."

Our Father. . . .

The Second Sorrowful Mystery:
Jesus Is Scourged

So Pilate, anxious to placate the crowd, released Barabbas for them and, after having Jesus scourged, he handed him over to be crucified.

— Mark 15:15

The Scourging at the Pillar from Fra Angelico (Guido da Vicchio, later Giovanni da Fiesole) (1378, Tuscany — 1455, Rome), the cells at San Marco.

Jesus Is Scourged

It would take a lot of courage for an artist, if he be not the most callous of persons — and then he would probably not be drawing a picture of the Savior — to bind the hands of our Lord even with ropes of pencil lead and to draw each one of his sacred wounds. It would put him excruciatingly in touch with reality.

For the reality is that we have bound the hands of the Lord, those hands that ever reach out to us in love, ever since they secretly and most lovingly fashioned us in the womb. The hands that would embrace us and heal us we tie with rough cords, lest we feel their most caring touch, our hearts melt, and we are forced to desist from our sinful ways. Our gentle artist would rather hide this painful ignominy behind our Savior's back to spare himself the pain and to spare us the painful confrontation with the doing of our obstinate self-centered love.

Nor could our gentle artist bring himself to disfigure the most holy body of his Beloved and ours with the gaping wounds that leather thongs and sharp iron tips would soon produce, each one convicting us of our heartless sinfulness. The wound of our pride. The wound of our gluttony and overindulgence. The wound of our lust and sensuality. The wound of our dishonesty and selfishness. And on and on. Our sins have never ceased, nor have they ceased to rip the body of Christ.

Rather here are we confronted with the lean naked body and the pleading eyes of love. Let us not mistake the pleading cry of those eyes. They do not say: Please, do not tear me to pieces. Oh, they do say that. After all he is a man, a man of flesh and blood, and his body and all his sensibility recoil from the impending agony. But more is his pleading for us, we who hold the whip, and we who have the freedom and means to scourge his most sacred body, to wound it in so many ways. His silent, loving pleading is for us — whom he loves so much. For he knows that each blow that tears his body, tears us even more profoundly. It does violence to the Body of Christ that we are. It does violence to our very nature, to the right order of the nature of one who has not only been most lovingly created as a creature of this God of love but has also and even more wondrously been baptized into the very Body of Christ.

As horrible as is the violence done to the body of our Savior by the whips of the burly Romans, as horrible as is the violence done to the Body of Christ by our sin, the greatest violence is done to our very own nature, to who we are, when we rebel against God and ourselves in sin. Or when, in our weakness, we betray ourselves and our God. Such is the love of this Man for us, the selfless love, that he suffers more from what we suffer than from what he himself suffers.

By his wounds we are healed. His sorrow-filled plea is that we do not whip him with our sin. Yet his love is such that he allows the tearing and scarring wounds of those whips to be the very healing of our sin. If only we let them be.

Perhaps we need more courage than the artist shows here; we need to let the reality of each of our Savior's gaping wounds be present and confront us. We do need to see that it is our hand that holds the rope that binds his loving, healing hands. Those hands for years had ceaselessly reached out in healing: lepers, the blind, the deaf, those who suffered violence — even the violence of his own chosen "pope." He only wants to reach out and touch us and heal us. But we, in so many ways, bind his healing love. We do not believe. We do not trust. We fear such love, lest it bind us even more tightly. For what other response can we give to such love, but total self-giving love?

In our selfishness and in our incomprehension we do not want to be bound by such love. We want to be "free" to do our own thing — our own shortsighted thing which we so foolishly believe to be the way to happiness. We do not understand that the only way to happiness for us is the way of self-giving love, of recklessly receiving all the love this Divine One would pour out upon us and with equal recklessness give all the love we have in return.

We hold the rope, though not with any firm determination, for his grace is in fact at work within us. We avert our eyes, lest we see his look of infinite compassion and love. It would melt us and we would immediately be converted.

As we pray this decade, let us have the courage to look into those eyes and even perceive the numinous of the Divine beyond them. Perhaps, just perhaps, we will then open to that grace, that he indeed wants to give us, that will hold back our arm so ready to strike, that will enable us to keep from inflicting any further wounds upon the One already wounded far too much, wounded for us and by us.

Our Father. . . .

The Third Sorrowful Mystery:

Jesus Is Crowned with Thorns

The soldiers led him away to the inner part of the palace, that is, the Praetorium, and called the whole cohort together. They dressed him up in purple, twisted some thorns into a crown and put it on him. And they began saluting him, "Hail, king of the Jews!" They struck his head with a reed and spat on him and they went down on their knees to do him homage. And when they had finished making fun of him, they took off the purple and dressed him in his own clothes.

— Mark 15:16-20

Jesus Is Crowned with Thorns
from Dirk van Baburen (1590-1624),
"Christ Crowned with Thorns" now in the Kansas
City Art Museum.

Jesus Is Crowned with Thorns

A big, burly, brute of a man ferociously forces the homemade crown down upon the sacred head. He does not want to get any more pricks from the vicious thorns. He has already gotten enough of them in plaiting this extraordinary crown. I wonder if ever another has worn such a crown?

With the broken pieces of reed, he forces the crown down onto the unprotected brow. The long thorns rip open the flesh, even as others force their way through the matted hair to do the same, and go deeper to press into the skull. I really cannot fathom what must have been the pain and agony that tore into this most sensitive soul. I think of the dizzying, numbing migraines I have had. And the throbbing fever headaches.

But these are nothing in comparison to what this Man now suffers.

But it is not only a question of physical pain. The soldiers had heard his declaration. Their commander, the righteous Pontius Pilate, had asked, with a certain derision masking a deep fear: *Then you are a king?* And he answered with an unnerving calm dignity: *You say that I am. For this was I born and for this I have come into the world. But my kingdom is not of this world.* He is a king . . . the king of the despicable Jews . . . this naked, tattered remnant of a man. Then he shall be honored as a king. The crown was plaited. A rough red cloak was found to drape over his shoulders, already made red with blood, torn by deep, gaping gashes. A reed for a scepter was forced into his bound hands. And then the show began. Creatures dared to assail their Creator. Hands that were lovingly fashioned in the womb struck the face of the one who so lovingly fashioned them. Knees bent in derision. Disgusting spittle punctuated even more disgusting words that debased truth and turned it into mockery. King of the Jews! Yes, and Lord of all creation. I wonder, when the moment of enlightenment came for these lusty young men, in this life or in the judgment, what must have been their reaction to the almost unbelievable sacrilege that they had perpetrated?

But are they to be so completely condemned? Are they not more sinned against than sinning? We have seen it again and again. Good young men plucked from their healthy home environment, shipped off to some camp where they are trained to be vicious killers and given the weapons to do it. Then they are transported to some far distant and wholly alien post and left with hours of boring routine. The deepest sadistic tendencies emerge. And what follows is not worthy of a human person. These young Romans had known many hours of emptiness and loneliness and suffered their share of derision at the hands of the Jews. Now the king of the Jews was in their hands. He may now be a tattered remnant of a man but he looked smart enough last Sunday when he rode into Jerusalem amid the cheering and adoring crowds. Then the cloaks were going on the ground to soften the fall of his donkey's step. Branches were waving and voices shouting glad Alleluias. *Hosanna to the Son of David.* Let this Son of David see what kind of royal authority he has inherited. *Hail, King of the Jews.* The smacks resound and the spittle flies in the wake of the sacrilegious words.

Before I even think of laying any condemnation at the door of these young Romans, let me first look at my own record. I do know and confess that this is indeed the Son of David, the

Son of God, the King of the Jews and my King. Yet, the way I so frequently act, is it not a mockery of his lordship over me? Is it not a mockery when I say to Jesus: You are my Lord and my God, and then, instead of doing what he wants, I blithely go on to do just what pleases me. I allow the boring routines of my life serve as an excuse for seeking "compensating" pleasures. I give him so little of my time and attention. He who asked, *Could you not watch one hour with me?* does he get even an hour of my time each day, not to speak of a tithe? If actions speak louder than words, how genuine and authentic is my homage of him as my King and God?

What reparation can I offer to him for all that he has suffered for me and from me, for what he suffers now as these brutes crown him and mock him? I can certainly offer my many headaches and the humiliations that come my way. I can offer, too, the many unwanted thoughts and images that invade my head like so many thorns. My mind and imagination are not wholly under my control. They just keep turning out their thoughts and images, even when I would that they be still and leave me at peace to worship and contemplate, or even simply to rest. I can develop a certain facility to let much of the constant mental chatter and shadow go by. But there are the painful thoughts and images that come to renew old pain and humiliation. They wring my soul again. And the thoughts that provoked that hatred and anger which I do not want. I do want to forgive and forget. I have forgiven. But the inner computer still holds the data and it mercilessly keeps coming up. And there is the lust, too, that would betray me and lead me to use others, betraying their openness and trust. Lord, have mercy. I am truly pierced by these thorns, and so many others. May your piercing be my healing. May my suffering and the offering I make of it in union with your crowning make some reparation to you for all you have suffered for me. May I grow in compassion for you and for all your suffering members. Even for these young Romans, and all who through the centuries, even to our own times, have had their own humanity so abused that they have become abusers. Help me, O Lord, to work and pray for total disarmament of mind and heart, of home and nation, till all this abuse ends.

Lord, I stand, I kneel, in true homage, before you, my Lord and King. I worship you and hail you as the true King of the Jews (May your people come to recognize and worship you!) and of us all. You have paid such a price because of all our pretensions, you the true King. Lord, have mercy.

Our Father. . . .

The Fourth Sorrowful Mystery:
Jesus Carries His Cross

As the soldiers were leading Jesus away they seized on a man, Simon from Cyrene, who was coming in from the country, and made him shoulder the cross and carry it behind Jesus. Large numbers of people followed him and women, too, who mourned and lamented for him. But Jesus turned to them and said, "Daughters of Jerusalem, do not weep for me; weep rather for yourselves and for your children. For look, the days are surely coming when people will say, 'Blessed are those who are barren, the wombs that have never borne children and the breasts that have never suckled!' Then they will begin to say to the mountains, 'Fall on us!' to the hills, 'Cover us!' For if this is what is done to green wood, what will be done when the wood is dry?" Now they were also leading out two others, criminals, to be executed with him.
—Luke 23:26-32

Simon the Cyrenian helping Jesus from Titian (Tiziano Vecelli) (1488-90, Piene di Cadore, Italy — 1576, Venice), "Carrying the Cross" in the Prado, Madrid.

Jesus Carries His Cross

How happy I would be to help Jesus carry his cross, to have the divine eyes rest upon me, to receive that look so full of love and compassion. Indeed I envy the Cyrenian.

But what were the dispositions of his mind and heart? Was he in some way a disciple? Did he realize what a privilege was his? Did he perhaps at that moment when the divine gaze rested upon him receive some enlightenment, like the good thief upon the cross? Or was he so filled with self-pity at having been dragged into this thing that he totally missed the grace of it? Was he so humiliated at being publicly identified with this poor wreck of a man, this public criminal, that he could think of nothing but himself?

There were others, of course, who entered into the drama of this sorrowful journey. John, the beloved disciple, was never very far away. His love compelled him to stay as close as he could, right to the end. Perhaps it was he who brought the virgin Mother. What a dreadful moment of encounter that was when first the divine gaze met the eyes of his Mother. Once Jesus said to one of his saints: If I had not made the world, I would make it just for you. He would certainly have said to Mary: If I did not need to die for anyone else, I would willingly die for you alone. But perhaps the greatest sorrow of his whole passion, after the crushing pain of standing before his Father with the guilt of all our sin, was for him seeing the pain and anguish in the eyes of his most dear mother. He willingly suffered to keep her free from all sin and all the consequences of sin. Yet in that same love he could not deny her the longing of a mother's heart to be with her Son in his most bitter agony. How mysteriously are love and suffering woven together by compassion — in the deepest meaning of that word.

There were other women, too. The courageous one whom we call Veronica, who pressed through the crowd and even pushed her way past the rough and burly guards to give a moment of refreshment to the Victim — far more refreshing because of the love it expressed than any physical comfort it afforded. The courageous kindness was rewarded so wondrously, a reward we have shared through the centuries: a true icon, the very image of our suffering Savior.

And those other women, less courageous, yet

nonetheless courageous enough to publicly show where their feelings lay. They received the compassion of a mysterious prophecy that would perhaps someday comfort them or the children they now held in their arms.

But it was a man — and I am not quite sure what exactly that is meant to say to us — who was allowed to enter most fully into Christ's most painful and wretched journey. Maybe it says that we less sensitive men need to be touched more physically by the pain of the Lord in order to respond and be with him in compassion. Maybe it intimates something about our role in the ongoing work of the redemption, of making the saving passion of Christ present in the world today. I can only think of how horrible must have been the pain our Lord was suffering as that heavy beam pressed down and lurched back and forth on those shoulders lacerated with innumerable open and burning wounds. To be able to lift off some of that burden, if not all of it, even for part of the horrendous journey! Such an intimate, powerful and poignant call to compassion, to *be with* our Beloved in his *passion*.

As I survey the scene from a safe distance my heart is deeply moved and there is a deep longing to be with the Lord, to be Simon the Cyrenian, to have the unique and immense privilege of helping our Lord carry his cross. And yet what happens when the distance is closed, when that cross is offered to me in my own daily life? Are my eyes of faith quickly blinded by my wallowing self-pity? Am I so humiliated and self-conscious that I lose all consciousness of the privilege that is being offered me? Do I totally forget that we are indeed called to *make up what is wanting in the passion of Christ?*

The first time I heard those words in the epistle of Saint Paul I wondered about them. What could be wanting in the passion of Christ? It was more than complete. It had satisfied for all our sin and more. What could be wanting in the passion of Christ? The mystery of it — that God wants the passion of Christ to be effectively present in our world today by our participation in it. Ours is the privilege, a costly one — as costly as it is sublime — to make Christ's passion and all its healing effects present to our brothers and sisters. And to ourselves, here and now by our living that passion in ourselves, by being like Jesus a complete "yes" to whatever the Father asks of us. "Yes" even when our human nature, like his, sweats blood and cries to be let off.

If I can only clearly see and keep in mind that the headache and the heartache that I am asked to bear with today is my opportunity to be Simon, to actually help Jesus carry his cross, to be intimately with Jesus in his passion — how much easier or, at least, more meaningful will be each of my daily crosses. May this be part of the grace that is woven into my life, into my consciousness, as I pray again and again this fourth sorrowful mystery.

Our Father. . . .

The Fifth Sorrowful Mystery:
The Crucifixion

The soldiers offered Jesus wine mixed with myrrh, but he refused it. Then they crucified him and shared out his clothing, casting lots to decide what each should get. It was the third hour when they crucified him. The inscription giving the charge against him read, "The King of the Jews." And they crucified two bandits with him, one on his right and one on his left.

The passers-by jeered at him; they shook their heads and said, "Aha! So you would destroy the Temple and rebuild it in three days! Then save yourself, come down from the cross!" The chief priests and the scribes mocked him among themselves in the same way with the words, "He saved others, he cannot save himself. Let the Christ, the king of Israel, come down from the cross now, for us to see it and believe." Even those who were crucified with him taunted him.

When the sixth hour came there was darkness over the whole land until the ninth hour. And at the ninth hour Jesus cried out in a loud voice, "Eloi, eloi, lama sabachthani!" which means, "My God, my God, why have you forsaken me?" When some of those who stood by heard him, they said, "Listen, he is calling on Elijah." Someone ran and soaked a sponge in vinegar and, putting it on a reed, gave it to him to drink saying, "Wait! And see if Elijah will come to take him down." But Jesus gave a loud cry and breathed his last. And the veil of the Sanctuary was torn in two from top to bottom. The centurion, who was standing in front of him, had seen how he had died and he said, "In truth this man was the Son of God."

There were some women watching from a distance. Among them were Mary of Magdala, Mary who was the mother of James the younger and Joses and Salome. These used to follow him and look after him when he was in Galilee. And many other women were there who had come up to Jerusalem with him.

— Mark 15:23-41

The Crucifixion
from Matthias Grünewald (1455-80, Würzburg —
1528, Halle, Germany), "The Crucifixion" (before
1616) central panel of the Isenheim (Athonite
Monastery) Altarpiece, based on the revelations of
St. Bridget of Sweden, now in the
Unterlindenmuseum, Colmar.

The Crucifixion

Has there ever been a sorrow like unto my sorrow?

Jesus asks in prophetic voice: Has there ever been a sorrow like unto my sorrow? And we must answer: Indeed, no. As we look upon him who has been pierced, what can we say?

This exquisitely beautiful body, the fruit of a virginal womb, of a sinless one, untouched by the blight of human sin, never has a body been more sensitive to pain. And now it is elongated in crucifixion, gasping for every breath. Every muscle already exhausted, yet it must strain for another gulp of air. And with each exertion the gaping wounds in wrist and feet wear and tear yet more around the cutting, rough iron of the nails. Flailed by more wounds than any can count as they crisscross one another, shredding the tender flesh. The mockery of the crown, emphasized by the sign overhead, King of the Jews, brings its own throbbing pain and piercing torture as the head is thrown back again and again in spasm against the rough wood. And the humiliation of his nakedness, exposing the very fragility of his manhood.

Beyond this is the deeper pain, that of the sinless one clothed in all sin. No human has ever comprehended the full malice of human sin, but this man-God. And knowing that malice, he stands before God, his Father, with the whole crushing weight of it upon him. No one has ever loved the Father as has this beloved Son. His love is the very person of the most Holy Spirit of Love. Yet that love is violated by all sin, now his sin. *Father, if it be possible, let this chalice pass from me.* If it be possible. Certainly it was possible. But love still asked. And love still gave.

No, there never has been any sorrow like unto this sorrow. And yet no artist dare try to depict it in all its horror. If one should dare to attempt it the picture would immediately be labeled garish or crude. Yes, it is crude, horribly crude, what has been done to this Man.

And we are confronted by it. It is time to leave off words. Rational analysis, images — what can they do but belittle it. It is beyond all these. We can only contemplate the reality, opening ourselves to the intuitions of Divine Love, allowing love to bring us beyond ourselves to experience that which transforms even if it is too much to inform — too much beyond our human receptive capacities to receive form.

As we allow this reality to be a presence within us, the Crucified Christ, we come to see its reflections, its shadows, its participated reality in the world all around us. We see the Crucified One in the despised African American whose humanity the arrogance of the White keeps nailed down. We see the Crucified One in the "lazy Indian" whose humanity has been truncated and numbed by a subhuman, corralled environment. We see the Crucified One in the "licentious gay" whose humanity, labeled and libeled and unaccepted by family, society, and church, cries out in its loneliness for compassion and relationship. We see the Crucified One in the ghettoized Jew who is set outside the city and the society by some distorted "Christian" instinct. We see the Crucified One in the disabled, who are not given a chance to reveal their true inner beauty and to use the splendid talents they do have from the Lord. We see the Crucified One in all the suffering, the despised, the segregated. We see, if we have eyes to see.

The longer we look upon him who has been pierced, the humbler we become. We come to know the leprosy of our own sin; how despicable we ourselves indeed are. We come to know we are one with the despised and crucified Christ and by his wounds we are healed. We come to know that we are in truth one with every wounded human, we are all wounded. We come to know *compassion*, we "suffer with." And there is no one whom we do not "suffer with."

We have moved with Christ through his mysteries, from his descent and self-emptying at the Incarnation, through his gestational and educational experiences, to the bloody steps of his passion. Now it is time to stop. To be. To leave off the parameters of our own thoughts and images. To be before the cross, wide open. And to let ourselves be invaded by the Divine in their most powerful expression of their compassion.

This fifth sorrowful mystery is indeed, the mystery for contemplation.

Our Father. . . .

The Five Glorious Mysteries

The First Glorious Mystery:
The Resurrection

When the Sabbath was over, Mary of Magdala, Mary the mother of James, and Salome brought spices with which to go and anoint him. And very early in the morning on the first day of the week they went to the tomb when the sun had risen.

They had been saying to one another, "Who will roll away the stone for us from the entrance of the tomb?" But when they looked they saw that the stone — which was very big — had already been rolled back. On entering the tomb they saw a young man in a white robe seated on the right-hand side and they were struck with amazement. But he said to them, "There is no need to be so amazed. You are looking for Jesus of Nazareth, who was crucified; he has risen, he is not here. See, here is the place where they had laid him. But you must go and tell his disciples and Peter, 'He is going ahead of you to Galilee; that is where you will see him, just as he told you.' " And the women came out and ran away from the tomb because they were frightened out of their wits; and they said nothing to anyone, for they were afraid.

Having risen in the morning on the first day of the week, he appeared first to Mary of Magdala from whom he had cast out seven devils. She then went to those who had been his companions and who were mourning and in tears and told them. But they did not believe her when they heard her say that he was alive and that she had seen him.

— Mark 16:1-11

The Descent into Hell
from Fra Angelico (Guido da Vicchio, later Giovanni
da Fiesole) (1378, Tuscany — 1455, Rome), the cells
at San Marco.

The Resurrection

His face is suffused with light, calmness, peace, and joy — a noble beauty. His hair flows now, no longer matted with blood, a tangled mass held in place by a crown, a crown of thorns. His whole being radiates. He is risen. Yes, he is truly risen.

He is beautiful, attractive, glorious. And we, too, shall be beautiful, attractive, and glorious. God delights in our beauty, a beauty that reflects his own. It is good for us to have care for our bodies, these temples he has given us. He wants us to rejoice in them, to care for them, to develop healthy habits and good training. "The glory of God is the human fully alive" (Saint Irenaeus).

He carries a standard of victory. And it is marked with the cross. Even his halo is marked with the cross. What was a few days ago a sign of ignominy and shame, an instrument of torture that profoundly debased the human, has become the triumphant sign of glorious victory. In this sign we shall conquer.

Even while we celebrate life, we must yet accept the cross — all the little crosses of our lives. Indeed, embrace them, and in embracing them embrace his now glorious cross. For all our crosses are transformed by his victory and have become for us the way to victory and glory.

Christ has risen. Christ has truly risen. And he has not risen only for himself alone nor alone. Saint Matthew tells us in his gospel that when Christ died "tombs opened and the bodies of many holy people rose from the dead, and these, after his resurrection came out of the tombs." Pope John XXIII, sitting upon his throne in his cathedral church of Saint John Lateran, literally *ex cathedra*, told us that it can piously be believed that Joseph, the husband of Christ's virgin Mother, was among these holy people and that they ascended with him into the heavenly places.

In the traditional icons of the early church we see Jesus, having "descended into hell," raise up Adam and Eve and lead them forth. Here our artist leaves us with a bit of ambiguity. There is but one pair of hands that grasp the liberating hand of the triumphant Savior. Is it Adam? Is it Eve? The fact is that in the Lord there is neither male nor female. Both have been resumed in their fullness. The risen Christ, into whom each one of us has been baptized — we were buried with Christ in the waters of baptism and rose up out of them into his risen life — calls us forth to the fullness of human life with its complete integration. He reaches to draw forth from us all the repressed dimensions of our being, to call us to live a full life in him. Again "the glory of God is the human person fully alive."

He is fully alive and all glorious, this risen Savior of ours. Yet we see unmistakably in his hand and in his foot, the mark of the nails. Not now grizzly, gaping wounds but rather glorious marks of victory. A great victory over sin and death, over the most sacrilegious of crimes, the most base of human deeds.

We see in ourselves the ravages of sin. If we do not die a young and sudden death, we will mark the diminishments that move us inexorably toward dissolution. Jesus allowed to be worked in his most perfect and sinless body all the ravages lusty and cruel people could work. He was totally wrecked until finally his very heart was pierced and the last drops of blood and water flowed forth. Thus he witnesses to the supreme power of his resurrection, as he rises all glorious and triumphant. Because he has risen, we too shall rise. *If he be not risen our faith is in vain.* But he is risen. And we shall rise. No matter what our sins and the sins of our parents and our people have wreaked in us, we too shall rise all glorious and beautiful. And what we have suffered for Christ and for others — *whatever you do for the least of my brethren, you do for me* — will leave its marks upon us, not disfiguring marks but marks of yet greater glory.

As we face the diminishments of life we want often to pray this decade and meditate on this mystery. In it is our sure hope and our confidence. For even now, our risen Lord reaches to us to raise us up in spirit and to make our faces shine with his joy and his peace. This is the beauty we see in the face of a Mother Teresa, that face so worn and furrowed with countless wrinkles yet compellingly attractive. This is the twinkle we saw in the eyes of John XXIII, the old man who knew many years of exile but ended up "on the top of the heap" with enough vigor to change the history of humankind. This is the light of the resurrection that would shine out of each one of us if we would but die to all the pretenses of our false self and simply be who we truly are — men and women baptized into the risen Christ, who has conquered death and all the effects of sin and stands before us, reaching out to us, with wounds all glorious. Let us reach out and clasp his hand in loving and trusting faith.

Our Father....

The Second Glorious Mystery:
The Ascension

Now having met together, the apostles asked Jesus, "Lord, has the time come for you to restore the kingdom of Israel?" He replied, "It is not for you to know times or dates that the Father has decided by his own authority but you will receive the power of the Holy Spirit which will come on you and then you will be my witnesses not only in Jerusalem but throughout Judaea and Samaria and indeed to earth's remotest end."

As he said this he was lifted up while they looked on and a cloud took him from their sight. They were still staring into the sky as he went when suddenly two men in white were standing beside them and they said, "Why are you Galileans standing here looking into the sky? This Jesus who has been taken up from you into heaven will come back in the same way as you have seen him go into heaven." So from the Mount of Olives, as it is called, they went back to Jerusalem, a short distance away, no more than a Sabbath walk.

— Acts of the Apostles 1:6-13

The Ascension
from Andrea Mantegna (c. 1431, Vicenza — 1506,
Mantua) Triptych (c. 1465) in the Uffizi, Florence.

The Ascension

There is something of a twinkle in the Lord's eye. He can hardly keep from smiling. Here he is sending off this motley crew of cowards, telling them to go forth and teach all nations. It was like the time he met Peter and called him "Rock" — the man who would quail before the questioning of a little servant girl. Yes, he chose the weak of this world, so that no flesh would glory in itself. Peter would become rock but only after he finally got in touch with his own weakness and his love. He had done a lot of stupid things; he had really failed his Lord. And he had wept. Now he was ready. And so were the others, more or less.

They still dreamed dreams: Lord, will you establish your kingdom at this time? Yes, they still saw themselves lording it over others in this world's fashion. They had not heard him declare to Pilate: *My kingdom is not of this world.*

For now, all they needed to do was to go into the city and wait for the Holy Spirit. The Paraclete, the Comforter, the Strengthener, the one who would make them strong and recall to their minds all he had taught them, would come to them ten days hence. They needed a retreat. They needed to reestablish their number, finding a replacement for poor Judas. They needed to gather around Mary, the Mother of the Church, and prepare for its birth — its birth in them. For that mystical Spouse who sacramentally came forth from his side on Calvary's hill, came forth in blood and water, was to actually come forth in them on Pentecost.

But they do not quite understand all this yet. They do not understand the share in his chalice that is to be theirs. So they stand here, clinging to him, if not physically like the women at Easter, certainly and more tenaciously in their hope and fear and, yes, love. They have come to love him very much, just as he loves them. *No longer servants, but friends.* This separation is difficult, but it is necessary. *If I do not go away the Spirit cannot come.* If everything is centered on the physical presence of Christ in one place, the mystical Body animated by the Spirit cannot grow and reach out to all the corners of the earth. The mission of the Head on earth is complete, now it is time for the

Body to be formed by the Spirit. And these men, this motley crew are to be the primary agents of the Spirit. These men and their apostolic successors are to head the Body on earth until it is complete and ready to ascend to be one with its Head in the eternal kingdom and glory of the Father.

Jesus has completed his mission on earth. He has lost none of those whom the Father has given him except that son of perdition. Now it is time for him to depart.

He has given his charge. He smiles. He blesses. And he quietly ascends. The apostles had seen many things. He had one day walked into each of their lives. He had called them. And they had responded. Though perhaps none of them could really say why. Certainly they had no idea what their response was going to lead to. He so often just disappeared from them. They learned to let that be. He wanted to have those nights alone with his Father. And he returned, sometimes even walking on the water or walking along a country road or walking through a closed door.

But now his going was different. They followed him with loving and longing eyes as he serenely ascended. There was a certain definitiveness about this departure. And there was something deep within each one of them that wanted to go with him, to ascend to where he ascended. He had promised: *I go to prepare a place for you.* But not now. For now, they had a mission. *Men of Galilee, why do you stand here looking up to the heavens?*

There is something deep in the heart of each one of us that stands, looking up to the heavens. We are, indeed, made for the heavenly kingdom. And we have been promised, we too, that a place is prepared for us. If we let go of all the superficial little wants to which we give much too much attention, we will come to be in touch with this great longing. And we will come to know that it can begin to be fulfilled, even now, as we turn within. *The kingdom of God is within.* And we will also come to realize that the way to its complete fulfillment is to be found in our now seeking to fulfill the will of God in our lives. God is where his will is. We must leave off at times our contemplation of heavenly things to go into the city and do what the Lord wants us to do. But may we never loose touch with the desire that is deep within us for Christ, to follow him into the heavenly kingdom. May we always have the desire to stand here in the idleness of contemplation, looking up to heaven. May this second glorious mystery bring us back here again and again.

Our Father. . . .

The Third Glorious Mystery:

The Descent of the Holy Spirit upon the Apostles

When Pentecost day came round, the disciples had all met together when suddenly there came from heaven a sound as of a violent wind which filled the entire house in which they were sitting and there appeared to them tongues as of fire: these separated and came to rest on the head of each one of them. They were all filled with the Holy Spirit and began to speak different languages as the Spirit gave them power to express themselves.

Now there were devout men living in Jerusalem from every nation under heaven and at this sound they all assembled and each one was bewildered to hear these men speaking his own language. They were amazed and astonished. "Surely," they said, "all these men speaking are Galileans? How does it happen that each of us hears them in his own native language? Parthians, Medes and Elamites; people from Mesopotamia, Judaea and Cappadocia, Pontus and Asia, Phrygia and Pamphylia, Egypt and the parts of Libya round Cyrene, residents of Rome — Jews and proselytes alike — Cretans and Arabs; we hear them preaching in our own language about the marvels of God." Everyone was amazed and perplexed; they asked one another what it all meant. Some, however, laughed it off. "They have been drinking too much new wine," they said.

Then Peter stood up with the Eleven and addressed them in a loud voice:

Men of Judaea, and all you who live in Jerusalem,

make no mistake about this, but listen carefully to what I say. These men are not drunk, as you imagine; why it is only the third hour of the day. On the contrary, this is what the prophet was saying:

In the last days — the Lord declares — I shall pour out my Spirit on all humanity. Your sons and daughters shall prophesy, your young people shall see visions, your old people dream dreams. Even on the slaves, men and women, shall I pour out my Spirit. I will show portents in the sky above and signs on the earth below. The sun will be turned into darkness and the moon into blood before the day of the Lord comes, that great and terrible Day. And all who call on the name of the Lord will be saved.

— Acts of the Apostles 2:1-21

John, Peter, and James the Less
from an unknown artist,
"Pentecost" — fourteenth-century miniature.

The Descent of the Holy Spirit upon the Apostles

God can never be deceived. Nor will he ever deceive, for he is, indeed, Truth itself. This is the ground of our faith.

God became man in Christ — Christ, the Way, the Truth, and Life. Before he completed his earthly mission and ascended to his kingdom, Jesus promised his Twelve that Holy Spirit, his Spirit, the Paraclete, the Comforter, Love would come upon them not many days hence. They were to go to Jerusalem to await her.

The Twelve understood now more clearly that they had a mission: Go forth and teach all nations, baptizing them in the name of the Father and of the Son and of Holy Spirit. As they gathered in the upper room awaiting the Paraclete, they were not the timorous little group who huddled there fifty days earlier, filled with sorrow, confusion, and pain. They were not exactly sure what Jesus' promise meant, just who this Holy Spirit was and how she would appear or come to them. But they believed. They had a mission. They rounded out their number, choosing a successor for Judas. They waited. Many came to wait with them. And in their midst, as an inspiring and steadying force was Mary, their life, their sweetness, and their hope. They prayed.

The Spirit came, came in power. And the Spirit came as one might have expected: in a mighty wind and fire. All the great theophanies of old were being fulfilled. The Lord, who descended upon Sinai in lightning and thunder, filling his people with awe and fear, made a covenant with them. Now a new covenant was established, a covenant written in God's own blood, shed on another mount, that of Calvary. The church that was born from the side of Christ on Calvary was now inspired. The church came forth to the world, to peoples of every nation, gathered together by divine design here at Jerusalem.

As the mighty wind embraced the house and shook it to its very foundations, tongues of fire came to rest upon the head of each. Each received Holy Spirit. And each in his or her own way.

A new and almost fierce determination shown

in the eyes of Peter. He was now ready to lead the Lord's little band forth to become a worldwide community of believers. The Rock was now rock, solid, firm, strong — no more cowardly denials would mar his total fidelity. Without hesitation he stepped forth, silenced the immense crowd gathering around the house, and spoke with power. He needed the help of the rest of the Twelve to baptize the thousands who came forth. Peter always needs the others to help him in his ministry.

James was no longer a "Son of Thunder." As the Spirit came upon him he went within to find a new peace and wholeness. He was to be the first of the twelve to drink the "cup" which the Master had drunk. His preparation for that had begun.

For his brother John it was another experience. He received the Love of his Beloved, this disciple whom Jesus loved. And he understood, as only the Spirit can make us understand, the secrets of Love: That the second command is like unto the first, that we are to love our neighbor as ourself. Not "love our neighbor as if she or he were ourself." No, our neighbor is ourself, we are truly one in Christ. When we fail to love our neighbor, we fail to love ourself. And conversely, if we do not love ourself, we cannot love our neighbor. In fact, there is only one Christ loving himself.

This is why we need deep prayer, that quiet

contemplative prayer where we see ourselves reflected back to us in the eyes of our God who so loves us. Only then do we see our own tremendous beauty and begin to love ourselves as we deserve. And at the same time we see that in this creative divine Love we are, indeed, one with all. We see the beauty of all. We love all as our self.

At this moment John also understood that other secret of love which Jesus had taught them: Whatever you do to the least of my brethren, you do to me. Again, the oneness. And John rejoiced that he could still do something for his Beloved. He went on to spend the rest of his long life doing just that. Above all and before all, he sought to share the secrets of love. "Little children," the old man repeated again and again, "little children, love one another."

Our God of love never ceases to pour out his Love. Each time we pray this decade we open our hearts to receive that outpouring, one with the whole church, which we are. And each time, each of us receives that Spirit of Love in the particular way that is appropriate to us and to where we are right now on our journey. We have but to open wide our hearts in waiting and expectant love, like the apostles, with Mary.

Our Father. . . .

The Fourth Glorious Mystery:
The Assumption of the Blessed Virgin Mary

Come, then, my beloved,
my lovely one, come.
For see, winter is past,
the rains are over and gone.
Flowers are appearing on the earth.
The season of glad songs has come,
the cooing of the turtledove is heard in our land.
The fig tree is forming its first figs
and the blossoming vines give out their fragrance.
Come then, my beloved,
my lovely one, come.
. . .
Come from Lebanon, my promised bride,
come from Lebanon, come on your way.
Look down from the heights of Amanus,
from the crests of Senir and Hermon,
the haunts of lions,
the mountains of leopards.
You ravish my heart,
my sister, my promised bride,
you ravish my heart with a single one of your glances,
with a single link of your necklace.
What spells lie in your love,
my sister, my promised bride!
How delicious is your love, more delicious than wine!
How fragrant your perfumes,
more fragrant than all spices!

— Song of Songs 2:10-13, 4:8-10

The Assumption
from Titian (Tiziano Vecelli) (1488-90, Piene di Cadore, Italy — 1576, Venice), "The Assumption" — Santa Maria dei Frari, Venice, now in the Academy.

The Assumption of the Blessed Virgin Mary

Saturday I spent some hours at the bedside of a friend dying of AIDS. I had had the privilege of receiving this fine young Jewish lawyer into the Catholic community three years ago. Now I sat there with his grieving parents and longtime partner, contemplating the ravages of death. For death had already taken hold of Steve. His and his loved ones' days of pain may be many more before death does finally claim its own. But what it has already worked in this beautiful young man is enough to tear any human heart.

Now I am flying over the virginal snows of the high Sierras. So pure, so untouched, so radiantly beautiful, washed by a strong, warming sun. God's plan untouched. Beauty, light, life, this is God's plan; not sin and death, corruption, and the grave.

Sin came into the world, and with sin death. Death, any form of death, is a terrible thing, the great penalty for our sin. And all the diseases that are a part of it. They tear the human person apart. They disfigure and destroy and lead to the complete disintegration of the human body, the exquisitely beautiful creation that was meant to harmonize so perfectly with the human spirit, together to reflect and hymn the divine beauty.

Jesus always did the things that pleased the Father. This was his passion. And it led him to his passion, and his death. And on to resurrection and ascension. God would not let his holy One see corruption. For us and for our salvation he knew sin and death. There was no sin in him, but sin worked all its havoc upon him as he took on the guilt of our sin. It scourged him and crowned him — with thorns — and nailed him up so that death could totally ravage him. But that was enough, and more than enough. The Father would not allow the grave to take its toll, to hold him captive. On the third day he rose, all glorious. His love wiped out sin, his death overcame death. His resurrection proclaimed a new promise. His ascension led the way. *I go to prepare a place for you.*

It was his Father, this same Father, who had decreed from Sinai's sulfurous heights that every son is to honor his mother. Could this Son, himself preserved from corruption, ever allow his mother, the Holy Virgin, to see corruption? Could he allow her most pure flesh from which he drew his own flesh, this body ever preserved as a most sacred temple, the ark of the new covenant — could he allow something so sacred to know the ultimate effect of sin? Could he allow death to celebrate its complete victory over her?

Everything in us says "No."

What son of a most loving mother would ever allow his mother to descend into the grave and know mortal decay if he had it in his power to keep her at his side in radiant beauty? Already Jesus had known sorrow enough in the pain he had caused his mother as he went forward to his divinely appointed mission. Leaving her alone in her widowhood, faced with the recriminations of uncomprehending relatives, was hard enough. Allowing her to walk with him to Calvary and to stand by his most torturous death-bed, a cruel consolation he could not deny her, cost him more than it cost her. Even if it was not due her, even if his filial duty did not demand it, the loving heart of this Son could hardly have borne to allow her to lie in corruption while he enjoyed all the bliss of the heavenly kingdom.

Come, then, my beloved,
my lovely one, come.

Whether Mary, like her sinless Son, experienced death or not, we do not know. The theologians argue this way and that. When Pope Pius XII solemnly proclaimed Mary's assumption, he was careful not to decide the question. The Scriptures are silent. We do not know. We do not need to know. What we do know is that, once Mary had completed her mission on earth, her Son sent his holy angels to bring this sacred ark of the new covenant, the body from which he received his body, to immediately share the glory of his own resurrected body.

He could not let his holy Mother see corruption. He could not allow the woman he loved most in all creation be anything but most beautiful. He had completed all the sorrows and pains of his mission. His heart was to be pained no more. Their separation, even in the flesh, had lasted long enough. Now that her mission was also complete, she was to be at his side in glory. She who had so valiantly stood by his cross would sit on his throne, just as close in glory as she had been in ignominy.

We who love Mary can only rejoice in this. We who know her as Mother want nothing less for her. We are happy that her Son has the power and the goodness to glorify her and to glorify her without delay. And we cry: *Look down from the heights.* ... Even as you enjoy the glory of your

Son and with him prepare a place for us, help us to come to that place.

The glory of the mother is the glory of her children. Mary's glory is Christ's glory. And it is our glory and our hope.

Our Father. . . .

The Fifth Glorious Mystery:
The Coronation of the Blessed Virgin Mary

Now a great sign appeared in heaven: a woman, robed with the sun, standing on the moon, and on her head a crown of twelve stars. . . .

The woman was delivered of a boy, the son who was to rule all the nations with an iron scepter, and the child was taken straight up to God and to his throne. . . .

As soon as the dragon found himself hurled down to the earth, he sprang in pursuit of the woman, the mother of the male chid, but she was given a pair of the great eagle's wings to fly away from the serpent. . . . Then the dragon was enraged with the woman and went away to make war on the rest of her children who obey God's commandments and have in themselves the witness of Jesus.

— Revelation 12:1-17

The Coronation of the Blessed Virgin Mary from Fra Filippo Lippi (1406, Florence — 1469, Spoleto), "The Coronation of Mary" (1441-47) Uffizi, Florence.

The Coronation of the Blessed Virgin Mary

From all eternity God had prepared Mary for him. And now she kneels before him. Kneels, bends the knee — for he is God, albeit man; and she is a creature, a product of his creative power, albeit the most beautiful and magnificent of all his creations, a creation worthy of the divine creative energies, a creation so far beyond anything any other creature can perceive or conceive, that she fairly seems to enter within the very borders of the Trinity itself.

She kneels, so graciously, so demurely — she is the very incarnation of humility. But only for a moment, till the divine hands which had fashioned her and given her all else, bestow upon her crowning glory: the crown of the Queen of Heaven and Earth, the crown of all creation, the crown of the consort of God. And then Christ raises her up, to sit her with himself on his throne.

One of my favorite mosaics in all the world is to be found in a twelfth-century church in the deeply impoverished section of Rome known as Trastevere. Santa Maria in Cosmeden was built when for the first time a Cistercian monk sat on the Throne of the Fisherman. And he was a holy man, too, Blessed Eugene III. This mosaic is unique in that it pictures Jesus and Mary together; but not now Jesus as a child or Jesus at Cana or Jesus in his Passion. But Jesus enthroned in glory. And there is Mary sitting at his side, sharing his throne. *And he has his arm around her*!

Mary has been tenderly and lovingly brought into a full sharing in her Son's reign over the creation he has redeemed. This should not surprise us. Did not God promise even to us poor sinners that we who open to Jesus' gentle knock, allowing his redeeming presence and love to flow into our lives will be given the victory and will sit with him on his throne even as he sits with his Father on his Father's throne? (Rev. 3) No one ever so completely opened to him as this woman who gave him her body and blood from which to fashion his very own human flesh and blood — the flesh and blood that would be sacrificed on Calvary and would feed us all in daily Eucharist.

Mary's sitting on that throne beside her Son is

no empty honor. He could never give such a model to the race he had redeemed. Woman is no mere adjunct to man, an ornament to complete the scene. Woman is a true equal, created to be man's helpmate, *like unto himself*. Jesus reigns as the Son of Man, a true man like unto us in all but sin. And he needs his woman at his side, receiving dominion, even as he does as man, from the Divine, albeit in a different way and through his mediation.

Mary participates fully in the reign of Christ, her Son. She is truly Queen of heaven and earth, of all creation. She has truly queenly power. And God has made her truly worthy of it and capable of exercising it.

The wondrous thing in this — for us — is that this woman, the pinnacle of God's created ones, the glory of all his creation, is our mother. And even in her sublime dignity and beauty and power, she bears within her bosom all the sentiments of a mother toward each one of us whom she bore in such anguish on Calvary's hill. Can a mother ever forget the child of her womb? Not this mother. In all her sublimity she yet regards each of us as her most dear child and cares for us most tenderly, even though she does not hesitate to use the fullness of her queenly power in our behalf.

As we behold the demure, all-beautiful and

untainted one present herself before the throne of Divine Grace to be crowned and raised to sit on that throne, we can wonder what we poor sinners, so stained with sin, have in common with our tainted nature's solitary boast. She is almost too young, too fair, too beautiful to be a mother. Yet she is mother, his mother and ours. And in all her sublimity that fact never ceases to be and to be most profoundly operative in all that she does.

We hail the Queen, knowing that she is mother, the mother of Mercy. And our mother — our life, our sweetness, and our hope.

Our Father. . . .

The Prayers of the Rosary

The Sign of the Cross
In the name of the Father and of the Son and of the Holy Spirit. Amen.

The Apostles' Creed
I believe in God, the Father almighty, the creator of heaven and earth and in Jesus Christ, his only Son, our Lord, who was conceived by the Holy Spirit, born of the Virgin Mary, suffered under Pontius Pilate, was crucified, died and was buried. He descended into hell. The third day he rose again from the dead. He ascended into heaven and sits at the right hand of God, the Father Almighty; from thence he shall come to judge the living and the dead. I believe in the Holy Spirit, the holy Catholic Church, the communion of saints, the forgiveness of sins, the resurrection of the body and life everlasting. Amen.

Our Father — The Lord's Prayer

Our Father, who art in heaven, hallowed be thy name. Thy kingdom come. Thy will be done on earth as it is in heaven. Give us this day our daily bread. And forgive us our trespasses as we forgive those who trespass against us. Lead us not into temptation but deliver us from evil.

Hail Mary — The Angelic Salutation

Hail, Mary, full of grace. The Lord is with you. Blessed are you among women and blessed is the fruit of your womb, Jesus. Holy Mary, Mother of God, pray for us sinners now and at the hour of our death. Amen.

Glory Be to the Father — The Doxology

Glory be to the Father and to the Son and to the Holy Spirit. As it was in the beginning, is now, and ever shall be, world without end. Amen.

The Fatima Prayer

O Jesus, forgive us our sins, save us from the fires of hell. Lead all souls to heaven, especially those who are most in need of your mercy.

Hail, Holy Queen — The Salve Regina

Hail, holy Queen, Mother of Mercy, our life, our sweetness, and our hope. To you do we cry, poor banished children of Eve. To you do we send up our sighs, mourning and weeping in this valley of tears.

Turn, then, most gracious Advocate, your eyes of mercy toward us. And after this our exile show unto us the blessed Fruit of your womb, Jesus. O clement, O loving, O sweet Virgin Mary.

Pray for us, O Holy Mother of God.
That we may be made worthy of the promises of Christ.

Let us Pray.
Pour forth, we beseech you, O Lord, your grace into our hearts, that we to whom the incarnation of Christ your Son was made known by the message of an angel, may by his passion and cross be brought to the glory of his resurrection, through the same Christ, our Lord. Amen.